Markets

Pamela Chanko • **Samantha Berger**

Scholastic Inc.

New York • Toronto • London • Auckland • Sydney

Acknowledgments

Literacy Specialist: Linda Cornwell

Social Studies Consultant: Barbara Schubert, Ph.D.

Design: Silver Editions

Photo Research: Silver Editions

Endnotes: Jacqueline Smith

Endnote Illustrations: Anthony Carnabucia

Photographs: Cover: Blair Seitz/Photo Researchers, p. 1: Lee Snider/The Image Works;
p. 2: George Haling/Tony Stone Images; p. 3: Frank Siteman/Tony Stone Images; p. 4: B. Daemmrich/
The Image Works; p. 5: Connie Coleman/Tony Stone Images; p. 6: Jon Gray/Tony Stone Images;
p. 7: Blair Seitz/Photo Researchers, Inc.; p. 8: J. Pickerell/The Image Works; p. 9: Michael
Busselle/Tony Stone Images; p. 10: M. Antman/The Image Works; pp. 11, 12: Suzanne & Nick
Geary/Tony Stone Images.

No part of this publication may be reproduced in whole or in part, or stored in a retrieval system, or transmitted
in any form or by any means, electronic, mechanical, photocopying, recording, or otherwise, without
written permission of the publisher. For information regarding permission, write to
Scholastic Inc., 555 Broadway, New York, NY 10012.

Library of Congress Cataloging-in-Publication Data
Chanko, Pamela, 1968-
Markets/Pamela Chanko, Samantha Berger.
p.cm. -- (Social studies emergent readers)
Summary: Simple text and photographs explore the variety of things that can
be bought and sold at markets around the world, including fish, fruits, cheese, and books.
ISBN 0-439-04554-1 (pbk.: alk. paper)
1. Markets--Juvenile literature. [1. Markets.]
I. Berger, Samantha. II. Title. III. Series.
HF5470.C48 1998
380.1--dc21   98-54352
                                                                          CIP AC

Copyright © 1999 by Scholastic Inc.
Illustrations copyright © 1999 by Scholastic Inc.
All rights reserved. Published by Scholastic Inc.
Printed in the U.S.A.

13 14 15 16 17   08   09 08 07 06

What do markets sell?

Markets sell bread,

and they sell flowers.

Markets sell meat,

and they sell fish.

Markets sell fruits,

and they sell vegetables.

Markets sell nuts,

and they sell cheese.

Markets sell old books.

Markets sell new toys.

Markets even sell candy!

Markets

A market is a place where some people sell things and others buy things. There are open-air markets, like the many farmers' markets around the country. Some markets are very small; others take up several city blocks. There are specialized markets that sell only one thing, like a bakery, and markets that sell almost everything, like a supermarket.

Bread Bakeries, supermarkets, and farmers' markets sell bread. Bread is one of the most important foods in the world. It is the basic food of most countries. All bread has two main ingredients, flour and water. From this base, hundreds of varieties of bread have developed around the world. Bakeries also make cakes, cookies, and pastries.

Flowers Flowers are sold in flower shops, in farmers' markets, and even in supermarkets. The biggest flower-growing country is Holland, which produces over half of all the flowers sold around the world. The flowers are carefully picked and packed into refrigerated trucks, trains, and planes and reach most markets within 24 hours—still looking fresh and smelling sweet!

Meat You can buy meat in the supermarket or in a butcher's shop. The U.S. is a big producer of beef and pork. Most meat is transported frozen to supermarkets and butcher shops. Meat inspectors check to make sure that the processing plants are sanitary and the meat is safe for people to eat. Butchers then cut and trim the meat for people to buy.

Fish Fish is sold in supermarkets and in fish markets. Most fish are caught with nets or fishing lines. Shellfish are dredged—nets or scoops are dragged along the ocean floor. Crabs and lobsters are trapped in special pots that are loaded with bait and then cast out to sea. In addition, some fish we eat are raised on fish farms. In markets, fish is sold fresh, frozen, canned, dried, salted, or smoked.

Fruits and vegetables Both fruits and vegetables are sold in farmers' markets and supermarkets. Refrigeration and fast transportation now allow us to import many fruits and vegetables so that we can eat them fresh year-round. Fruits and vegetables from the farmers' fields must be washed, trimmed, sometimes waxed, and packaged before they arrive at markets.

Nuts You can find nuts at all kinds of markets. Nuts are one of the oldest foods. Before people knew how to grow food, they lived mostly on nuts, roots, and berries. Different varieties of nuts grow around the world. Nuts are sold raw, with or without shells, roasted, salted, colored, or waxed.

Cheese Cheese has been produced all over the world for many centuries. Today most of the 200 varieties of cheese are made from cow's milk, but cheese is also made from the milk of goats, sheep, reindeer, and buffalo. Milk is left to stand in a warm place until it goes sour, and then it separates into two parts: a thick part called curd and a thin, watery part called whey. The curd is the part that eventually becomes cheese. The curd is then salted, pressed into its shape, and aged for various lengths of time.

Books Many cities have outdoor flea markets. There, you can browse among used clothes, dishes, furniture, and just about everything else you can think of. Flea markets often sell used books at very good prices.

Toys You can buy toys at a market, too! Some toys are very new, like robots and video games. Other kinds of toys are very old. Though the modern versions may look different, all through history children have played with dolls, tops, little toy weapons, toy soldiers, toy animals, vehicles, and boats.

Candy Markets sell candy in all shapes and flavors. The basic ingredient in candy is sugar that has been boiled or melted. Other ingredients, such as butter, corn starch, and flavorings, are added. The candy is poured into shapes, cooled, and then coated.